Get In the Game

The Ultimate Game Plan for Transition from College to Career

Matt Crevin

Voice of the Box Productions

www.VoiceoftheBox.com
© 2012

Get In the Game: The Ultimate Game Plan for Transition from College to Career

Address inquiries regarding coaching, training and volume orders to Matt Crevin at matt@voiceofthebox.com

ISBN 13: 978-0-9854346-0-1
ISBN-10: 0985434600

Publisher: Voice of the Box Productions
Editor: Deborah Drake
Cover Design: Jon Knight (www.soundpnp.com)
Interior Layout: Jon Knight (www.soundpnp.com)

Printed in the United States of America
First Edition 2 4 6 8

Dedication

I dedicate this book to my two boys Jake and Charlie. You inspire me to be the best person I can possibly be. Remember to follow your dreams and be ready when your opportunity comes! Above all, as you grow up; remember that no matter where you are or what you do, I love you.

Acknowledgements

There are so many people I should thank and if I started to list them all, I would no doubt leave someone out. I will always be grateful to the 49ers PR staff of 1991-92. Jerry, Rodney, Dave, Darla and Al (and Ricky S. too) They were all such a great team to learn from and were instrumental in my growth as a young professional. Of course I'd like to thank my parents, who always provide just the right guidance and support. I'd like to thank my editor Deborah Drake and designer Jon Knight, without their help this book would never have become a reality.

I would also like to say a special thank you to all of the guest contributors to my book. Their willingness to share their wonderful advice and guidance to the next generation is much appreciated. Most important of all, I'd like to thank you, the sports industry hopeful for taking the time to read my book. I wrote it with only you in mind.

Introduction

Many a professional athlete has transitioned from player to other roles within the industry, but what about the rest of us?

What about those of us who love sports (and have since youth), played well, didn't go "pro" and would love to put our love of the game and our professional skills to work within the sports industry?

What is the sports industry really made of? The sports industry is so vast and most people look at their favorite team as the place to work. But if you pull back to 10,000 feet you will see that it is more than your favorite team. It an industry with numerous career opportunities and needs as an organization, a company, a business that needs more than the star players and coaches to be successful.

This book has been a few years in the making. I look forward to sharing my 19 years of experience, unique perspective, my profound sports industry connections, rare insider interviews and extraordinary access with you. If you are passionate about pursuing a career in the sports industry, then this book is for you.

At the end of the day, the goal of this book and the collective wisdom contained within, is to both show and tell you how to make a successful career in sports for yourself!

I consider myself fortunate to be doing work I enjoy and care about, 19 years and counting. And this book is my way to open a door for those who would walk through it and create their professional dream.

We all deserve to be doing work that we enjoy, that uses our full bank of talents, and sometimes opportunities exist that we overlook because we limit our thinking about what is needed and what is possible.

Are you ready to start thinking beyond the game?

Foreword

by Rodney Knox

I first met Matt in 1992 when he came to the 49ers' offices for his internship interview. As was often the case with college students that would meet at our headquarters, they would be overwhelmed the moment they walked in. The trophy case with all the Super Bowl trophies and collection of rings would strike an imposing backdrop. NFL players walking around the complex also created a sense of star power that is tough to absorb right away.

Right away, what I noticed about Matt was that he did not appear to be awestruck. He was composed and was able to communicate very effectively why he would be a good choice as that year's PR intern. As it turned out, he was right and we hired Matt as the PR intern for the 1992 season. That season was a huge success on the field and in the front office and Matt was able learn firsthand and on the fly, what it takes to be part of a winning team.

Since that season, I have witnessed Matt's dedication to learn as many facets of the business of pro football as well as the sports industry as a whole. His dedication is evident by his commitment to the 49ers and his relationship with the team that has spanned 19 years, and counting. His hard work and willingness to do any assignment I gave him really helped his cause. I recall the season in which we gave Matt the responsibility to work with as many of the TV and Radio broadcast teams as possible because we knew Matt was consistently up to the challenge of the high-pressure environment that is always part of a live broadcast.

I have personally witnessed his passion grow over the years and now as founder of his own company, Voice of the Box, Matt has found a way to share his passion, knowledge and experience with others. He was recently on the Nike campus to interview a Sr. Director of global marketing and handled the interview with the ease and professionalism that I have witnessed many times before, just a lot more polished since his intern years! Matt brings a fresh and unique perspective to his work and always maintains the highest level of integrity along the way.

Since 1992, Matt has utilized his experience, knowledge and contacts in the sports industry and is now turning around and sharing his knowledge with the next generation of sports industry hopefuls.

"Get in the Game" is unique in many ways. It provides industry hopefuls with a great set of tools, ideas and concepts anyone can implement right away to help achieve their desired outcome. Matt combines his own 19 years of sports industry knowledge along with his 17 years of corporate experience to bring to the forefront experience, knowledge and action items that anyone can implement with ease, and better yet, that bring results. Now, more than ever, the information Matt provides is needed. He is a valuable resource as a mentor and **"Get in the Game"** should be required reading for anyone who is looking to make their break into the sports industry.

Rodney Knox,
Beaverton, OR

Rodney Knox is presently Senior Director of Communications for Team Sports at Nike, Inc. During his tenure as Director of Public Relations with the SF 49ers (1984-2003) the team won four Super Bowl titles.

Table of Contents

Pre-game

I remember the drive like it was yesterday. Leaving my apartment in San Jose, CA and heading to Santa Clara. The drive normally takes about 15 minutes but on that day back in 1992, it seemed to take 30 seconds. Excitement? Perhaps. Floating on a cloud? Pretty much. My mind was wandering all over the place on the drive to 4949 Centennial Blvd. There was no glut of sports radio to help pass the time, just me and my thoughts in my old Toyota Celica. I arrived at the San Francisco 49ers headquarters and my pulse started to quicken, palms starting to moisten. Noticing parking stalls reserved for team president Carmen Policy, team owner Eddie DeBartolo and head coach George Seifert did nothing to calm my nerves.

I somehow managed to navigate the parking lot full of high-end luxury cars without bumping a single one. I stood at my car for a few minutes to let the fresh air blow over me, to straighten my posture and to make one last check that my (only) sport coat and tie were in the best alignment possible. First impressions are important and I did not want to leave anything to chance. I gathered my notebook and walked with a sense of purpose into the lobby. I thought the fresh air from outside helped to calm my nerves, which it did until I entered into the lobby.

The first thing you see that almost jumps out off the walls when you walk in the building is the impressive trophy case. I have always enjoyed the rich history of the NFL, and growing up in the SF Bay area it was hard not to be aware of the 49ers amazing amount of success. Many bay area fans almost took that two-decade period for granted.

So when I walked in and took in the view of that beautiful trophy case with, at that time, four Super Bowl trophies, a sampling of championship rings representing the four world titles, mixed in with all the George Halas NFC Championship trophies, I was positively overwhelmed. I just walked in to the most blissful sports experience of my young life. The perspiration started to creep out of my palms once again. My hands regained dryness, for the time being. As I waited patiently in the lobby for a representative of the public relations staff to meet me, I noticed some of the 49er players walking around the corner into the players' entrance.

Out of one eye, I notice Joe Montana...JOE MONTANA, arguably one of the best quarterbacks in NFL history. Perspiration overdrive! Soon after, I catch a glimpse of Jerry Rice, then Steve Young, Brent Jones, Bill Romanowski, Tom Rathman, and defensive tackle Ted Washington, who looked a bit larger than the already "normal" size player. It seemed like an hour went by as I waited to go upstairs but it was really only five minutes, enough time to compose myself, yet again. My contact on the PR staff greeted me and he brought me upstairs to the offices.

As I walked up the circular staircase I was peeking at all the great artwork and photography adorning the walls. It was like a mini 49er hall of fame with fantastic pictures and memorabilia depicting the team's greatness. And then, I saw Dwight Clark walk by as I was heading into the Public Relations offices. Clark, along with Montana and the rest of the 1981 49ers was responsible for starting the 49er dynasty with the play that is simply called "the catch." I got settled into my chair before the interview started and quickly told myself, OK, I've seen a lot in just 10 minutes of being here. Relax and be yourself or else they will dismiss you right away. Remember what it is you want."

A sense of calm came over me and I decided to just have fun with this experience and let it flow. Thank goodness I had that brief moment of clarity for it served me well and was the first of many learning moments to come.

Learning Moment #1

You may be in awe of someone but when faced with the opportunity to be in the same room with him or her, do not let them see that. Respect them of course but do not be a super fan, just act as if you are going to be a peer of theirs someday (soon) and then they will respect you for that and you will earn their trust soon after. This method has helped me through many encounters like the one I had on my interview day. The "act as if" you are peer of theirs will allow your true personality and abilities to shine through from that point forward. You just need to "act" that way to get your foot in, wedged in the door, and then you are in.

The interview process was not a cakewalk but compared to the waiting downstairs in the lobby, it was fun. After the face-to-face interview portion was complete, I was given a tour of the facility and remember going into the coach's offices and being introduced to a few coaches on the 49ers staff that have since moved on to enjoy great success. Mike Shanahan (two time Super Bowl winning coach with the Broncos) and Jeff Fisher (17 years as the head coach with the Titans) to name a few. I walked through the locker room and out to the practice field where I met the rest of the PR staff and got to watch the remainder of the morning practice session.

I was hooked. I knew right then and there on the spot that this is what I wanted to do and this was the team I wanted to work for.

More than a few lessons came out of that first interview experience that eventually led to my being hired as the intern that year. Here is the short list for now.

Learning Moment #2

Interpersonal communications. Understanding the art of having a two-way conversation and being genuine about it is critical. Develop the ability to look someone in the eye and manage the 4 "C" playbook. Speak *clearly*, *concisely* and deliver a confident message, and be sure to always end with a clear *call to action.* Be authentic to the point where you really answer interview related questions the way you feel, as opposed to answering questions with replies you feel the interviewer is looking for. More times than not, showing your true colors, your vision of how you can do the job and add real value, is worth more than simply regurgitating stock answers all hiring managers have heard before.

Another strategy: Think clearly about how you would do a good job, what you would plan on doing AND share why you are interested in doing the job. Often times it is the "why" that motivates someone to hire you.

Able to stand on my feet in any social or professional situation and strive to do your best to be comfortable in your own skin. Trying too hard to impress, while you are networking or interviewing will come off the wrong way almost every time. There might be a time when you get flustered by a question;

simply take a deep breath, relax and "hit it" straight on. Being honest is always the best policy, just like mom used to say, right? If you are unsure of how to answer a question based on your perceived lack of knowledge or understanding of the topic at hand, it is always a good idea to be upfront, acknowledge the question and state, "I do not have experience to back me up but I feel confident that with good on-boarding and solid mentoring, I would be able to address this topic, get up to speed quickly and continue to learn, improve and deliver results."

The ability to listen more and talk less *(big ears small mouth).* Too many people today worry so hard and focus only on what they are going to say next that they do not co-actively listen and miss a great opportunity to take a conversation to the next level. Be a co-active listener. If you can truly listen to someone you have the ability to take any conversation and relationship to the next level, which is what you want. It might take you off your "scripted" list of questions but more times than not you will have plenty of chances to come back and ask those questions at a later time. A great example of this is what I learned from one of my former, and favorite Public Relations Directors with the 49ers, "KR"

Big Ears Small Mouth:

"KR" had told me stories about his former boss while he was with the Public Relations staff with the St. Louis Rams and mentioned it more than a few times: DO NOT be the one person in the office that talks out of turn, or the one that tries too hard to be the office gossip board and then in turn, pass the info around the office fueling rumors, etc. Having big ears and a small mouth is a wonderful phrase, which is a great skill that more people should implement. Listen, listen and listen some more. There will always be an appropriate time to share information, just be patient. *Quick Timeout:*

Do you need to be an athlete to work in the sports industry?

Short answer, no. But it does help to have the skill set of "playing well with others."

Certainly my athletic background was a help--but not in the way you might think. Many hiring managers like the fact that a candidate has an athletic background on some level. But not for the pure fact that they played sports, more importantly that they know the value of teamwork and that they can collaborate with others to reach a common goal. I was fortunate to have a few experiences at a young age that really helped form these core values in me.

At the age of 14, I traveled, by myself, to England to take part of the Sir Bobby Charlton Soccer Academy. (For those who may not know who Bobby Charlton is, he was a legendary Premiere League soccer player for Manchester United and captained the England national team in two world cups, winning the World title in 1966).

The experience I had while in England taught me so much more than how to be a better soccer player. I was thrust into a situation that included bunking with roommates from Belfast, Ireland as well having new teammates from all over England across different social-economic classes. My learning experiences were many, but being placed into a new scenario, in a different country and having the ability to adapt quickly, communicate effectively with a wide variety of people was a huge part of that particular experience being a positive, life changing event for me.

I was an all league soccer player in high school and then transitioned my skills into a successful international rugby career that spanned nine seasons. I earned individual awards but the team championships were the best memories I will have forever. Being part of the USA Maccabiah team that played in the 1991 Pan Am Games in Uruguay is certainly a highlight as well as a privilege. I got to play in five countries including playing a full season in New Zealand, arguably the top rugby country in the world. But it was not that I played competitively or what team I played on or the amount of success I had on the field that made the difference, although it is always a great icebreaker to jumpstart a conversation. It was the fact that I have been part of teams that were all pulling for the same goal. That, as it turned out, was a big factor.

Certainly my competitive spirit and drive to win did not hurt but it is more important how individuals go about winning that employers look for. Having the ability to communicate effectively with anyone in any given scenario is probably the top of most hiring managers wish lists.

1st Quarter
The "Internship"

Game Time! - 49er Internship

When I first got word that I was selected for one of the two PR internships for the 1992 season, I was ecstatic. When it finally sunk in Bay Area and having watched Montana work his magic as a kid from the comfort of my parent's living room couch, it was a dream-like scene playing itself out in living color. After that first encounter and introduction to the future hall of famer, I relaxed and got going with the process of "earning my stripes."

Those first few weeks of the internship, my head was spinning and everything seemed to be moving at warp speed. Just like athletes say, "in the pro's, the competition is bigger stronger and everything moves faster." I can tell you this much, all that is true and it also rings true for front office jobs too. But like any new role, it does get better after the initial acclimation period.

During my internship year, my manager provided an excellent opportunity to observe, learn and absorb as much as possible about all the day to day duties of the Public Relations department. The 49ers were not only loaded with talent on the field but also upstairs in the front office too. Partnering with and learning from the rest of the PR staff was fantastic and as soon as they saw I was willing to put maximum effort into my non-paying role, the more willing they were to help, the more accommodating and friendly they were in assisting me in my professional growth.

As the summer training camp concluded and the real season was fast approaching, I could feel the energy in the building pick up some serious momentum. With the 49ers, it was a mind set of anything less than a Super Bowl victory was a failure. That mindset also held true for all front office support staff. It was inspiring to be part of a work environment like this right out of the gate. What it taught me was to be prepared to work hard, take direction and have pride in what I did. It also taught me that as an intern, it is vital to do all the small tasks with pride and never consider any assignment too small to give it your all.

Many internships are loaded with small, and at times thankless assignments, but if you can show management that you will willingly handle them and complete them with pride, you will be given more and more responsibilities which will ultimately help you grow into any role. With the 49ers still being one of the top teams in the NFL at the time, the media spotlight was shining bright on them and with that came weekly national media coverage which meant all the top TV, Radio and print journalists were parading around the facility each and every week.

As the PR intern, I was given partial responsibility to assist them on their prep meetings leading up to a Sunday game. Great news for me as I was now rubbing elbows in a professional setting with the likes of TV titans Chris Berman of ESPN, Al Michaels from ABC, Joe Theismann and Mike Patrick of TNT, Dick Enberg and Bob Trumpy of NBC (OJ Simpson too) as well as the crew that worked with John Madden and Pat Summeral of CBS (soon to be FOX) I also got to partner with sports Radio legends like the late Bill King, Harry Kalas, Jack Snow as well as living legends like Marv Albert, Sonny Jerguson, Sam Huff, Matt Millen, Boomer Esiason Ted Robinson and many more.

What did this teach me? Well, a lot actually but the main learning moments are to be prepared, be ready to do whatever someone needs and just like the players on the field, be ready to go for an entire game (take no plays off!) Being in the broadcast booth during any live, unscripted event is a major adrenalin rush and for the first few times it is very challenging. Games on average last around three and half hours and you need to be dialed in and laser focused the entire time.

That entire intern season I worked predominantly as a spotter for the announcers. I would stand directly in between the play-by-play and color analyst and silently provide information on each and every play from scrimmage to the announcers via pointing to a master flip chart. Who made the catch, who made the tackle, who was the penalty on, who is the third receiver that just came in, who was the extra defensive back that came into the game, who recovered the fumble, who made the special teams tackle on the punt team and much more--which is a lot to do in a live unscripted and fast paced broadcast.

I remember the first time I was assigned to work with the Rams radio broadcast team. I was to work with the late great Jack Snow--one of the many broadcasters I watched during their playing days. I walked into the broadcast booth, introduced myself and the first thing he said, even before hello, was; "Are you any good?" He was poker-faced so my immediate reply was, "I'll be as good as you want me to be." He extended his former All Pro hand out for a shake and said, "You'll be just fine with me kid!" It is that kind of mental gymnastics that happens all the time. Working with professionals at any level and especially those that have played the game and have a decent sized ego for me was always interesting and fun work.

Learning Moment # 3

"Be prepared--at all times." As nice as it is to be given an assignment with time to prepare, it is truly a test of nerves, skill and agility to be handed an assignment with little or no time to prepare and still have the capacity to jump in and get it done. In many instances, this will be the case within the sports industry, especially live events. Be ready, be flexible and be prepared for just about any task that may come your way. You can get a jump on a rough idea of what to expect by asking good questions during informational meetings or interviews about game-day activities as well as non game-day activities. This will give you enough to go on in terms of the many moving pieces that you may be called on to handle.

Being flexible is an understatement but will certainly help you, as you just never know what you might be asked to do. This may seem obvious but many people, especially in today's work place, lack the concept of earning your stripes and doing whatever is asked of you and doing it well. Ask questions. No one will ever fault you for asking a question or inquiring to clarify an assignment. If you do not ask questions, managers will assume you understand and might find it bothersome if you go back after the fact to ask questions.

Asking questions on the front end will also show you have the desire to learn. Be sure to introduce yourself to others you naturally come in contact with and if the timing is right, you can ask them questions too. This will help you to better understand the bigger picture and how your specific role fits into the larger scheme. Having a decent snapshot of the overall big picture of whatever industry niche you pursue will serve you well. It is very easy to get drawn in to the granular aspects of your specific role-- for the obvious reason of wanting to grasp it as well as being good at it. But having a clear view of the big picture will help you be successful in your specific role because you will know how you, your role and what you are doing in your role all fit into the big puzzle.

I'll use pro football for example. Each week, for the most part is the same during the season. It one of the most structured routines in sports. Monday the players come in to get medical treatment, watch film while the head coach has his press conference. Tuesday is the player's day off and those that have any form of community involvement will do their community outreach on Tuesday. In the front office, (PR) a lot of work is done updating the player's bios with stats and getting prepped for the next game. What happens the rest of the week depends on whether the next game is a home or away game. A wide range of details are constantly updated for web use and put together for the broadcast teams (radio and TV) and local and visiting media need to be credentialed just to list a few items on the weekly checklist. Now this is just for the Public Relations Department.

When I was interning, I looked around the building to get a feel for what other departments did each day of the week to give me a broader perspective of the entire operation.

- Scouting

- Video operations

- Marketing

- Ticket sales

- Equipment and medical staff

- Security

And there are many other departments that comprise the whole organization.

While this is never as easy as I am making this out to be, when the time is right, it will prove to be beneficial to know what is going on around you. To see how your role and what you are responsible for fits into the big picture will be enlightening.

2nd Quarter
Game Day

NFL Game Day

Simply put, there is nothing quite like game-day in any given sport. I think it is heightened a little more for football because there is a week in between each game and the natural energy that builds up during the week creates a truly electric atmosphere on Sundays. After 19 years, I still get the same rush of energy as I drive to the stadium, park my car and walk through the players' entrance to get into the stadium. I still get the same feeling of excitement when I see the green grass of the field and stop to think that I may meet some very influential people in the sports business and I might be witness to something on the field on any given Sunday that has never happened in pro football.

To be privy to see what actually takes place behind the NFL curtain each Sunday across every stadium in the NFL is extraordinary. Visualize a three ring circus with all the moving parts, toss in 75,000 fans, 7,000 part time stadium staff, 400 members of the media, (TV and Radio production teams), local and visiting members of the print and on line media, team owners and VIP's and an assortment of related personnel all converging in one place for a three hour event. The good Public Relations teams make it look easy, which it clearly is not. Having witnessed the 1992 49ers staff, which at that time had been together for 10+ years was an ideal learning environment for me. The PR team needs to be extremely organized with all the segments I listed above, and they also need to manage the game-day timeline for the players. This includes when they need to be on the field and lined up for player introductions to the timing of the national anthem to all the post game activities.

The post-game schedule is usually more critical due to the fact that after the NFL mandated 10 minute cool down period (where the locker room doors remain shut to the media) the PR staff is closely monitoring all interview requests and facilitating key players to the podium room where they conduct in depth interviews to the media.

I can recall many instances of being inside the locker room before the doors opened to the general media (during the cool down period) after a 49er loss, it was as if a train wreck just took place, there were no casualties but everyone was walking around in stunned silence. These are the scenes that very few get to see.

Thankfully, in my first ten years, there were not too many Sundays where the 49ers lost. But one specific Sunday where they did lose comes to mind: The 1992 home loss to the Dallas Cowboys in the NFC Championship game. With a Super Bowl berth hanging in the balance the 49ers suffered a tough loss. My post game assignment that day was to go in to the 49er locker room and capture what are called immediate post game comments. Three players on offense or defense who had a big game, were involved in a key play or otherwise had a impact on the outcome. That assignment was hands down the toughest role I have ever had. The locker room that day was like the scene of a car crash with the exception of no fatalities. The only sounds were those of the showers running, helmets and cleats being tossed into the metal lockers, pads being removed from spent athletes and the sounds of miles of white athletic tape being removed from the players bodies with a special knife that slices it off without damaging the skin on the player...it is a most distinct ripping noise.

Knowing I had to secure at least two interviews, I was a bit timid approaching a player who just spilled his guts on the field and to then ask him tell me what happened. I migrated to the linebacker's section of the locker room and had my sights on Mike Walters. He was a well tenured player and one of the most approachable athletes I've been around. If it weren't for him, I'm not sure if I would have secured any post game comments. The **learning lesson** for me was this: Although it may seem to be a no win situation to go up and talk to a player who just suffered a tough defeat, do know that in the back of their minds, they understand that being respectful to the co worker or member of the media is part of their responsibility. Be firm with what you need to accomplish but of course be highly aware of your surroundings.

Do you need to be an athlete to work in the sports industry? Part 2.

Short answer, no. But it does help to have the skill of "playing nice with others" and having some background in competing to achieve the desired outcome. Plenty of lessons can be learned as an athlete of any level but if you do not have that set of experiences in your background, you are not completely out of the running. There are many other ways to showcase your skill sets by detailing any volunteering you have done, and internships you have held and more importantly what job functions you performed individually as well as collectively as part of any given work group (team). How did you collaborate with other groups to unite towards a key objective? How did you organize you work day or assist others in planning their workday, meetings and schedules? Are you a planner, or are you better suited to executing the plan that others developed? Whatever practical experiences you have gained, package it and position it towards the industry/company/role you are seeking.

If you do have some athletic performance in your background, be sure to include it in summary and if you have never competed as an athlete, be sure to detail your one key asset as well as the many other components of your background, skill sets and practical experience to showcase that you know what it takes to get any given job done with great results.

Certainly my athletic background was a help but not in the way you might think. Many hiring managers like the fact that a candidate has an athletic background on some level. But not for the pure fact that they played sports, more importantly that they know the value of teamwork and that they can collaborate with others to reach a common goal. I was fortunate to have a few experiences at a young age that really helped me.

Having the ability to communicate effectively with anyone in any given scenario is probably on the top of most hiring managers wish lists.

Assessments / Self assessments (Pre-game checklist)

Don't we all embrace the questions that family members and close friends throw at us at family gatherings? "So, tell me what you are up to these days and what are going to do for work now that you are close to graduating/or now that you recently graduated"? For many, we dread this most basic of questions. Even when we know it is coming, we cringe at how we are supposed to answer it when we know deep inside we have no clue. The most common response is to dig deep to create some form of reply that will buy us some time and make it sound as though we are on the right career search path. Another approach to this most common scenario would be to be honest and straight forward with your reply. Explain that you are spending a great deal of time researching the best options that fit nicely with your area of study or area(s) of interest.

You should always close that answer with, "Do you happen to have any thoughts/input/advice or contacts I can connect with that can assist me?"

You have got nothing to lose and plenty to gain by asking this very simple question and you never know what may come out of it. There have been many times I have asked this very question to friends and family and many times it has led to me being introduced to a new contact. **Don't be afraid to ask.**

As part of my most basic intake questions I utilize during my 1:1 coaching sessions, I pose to my clients, "What types of activities give you energy versus what types activities sap you of your energy." For many, that question stirs up a lively conversation and allows my clients to take stock of their goals in a different manner. Such basic areas to look at, as an example, would be the first area I tend to explore with all of my coaching clients: Do you enjoy working and collaborating with people either individually or in groups? Or do you prefer to be in a behind the scenes type of a role?

To look at what type of work environment or work setting suits your personality first will give you a big edge as you start to narrow your scope into a specific industry within the sports world. Taking the Myers Briggs assessment (or any newer version of personality type assessments) is also a good idea if you have never taken one.

These types of work-personality assessments are all aimed at giving you the best possible insight as to what areas are best suited for your specific personality type and work preferences. Being armed with this information will greatly enhance your search process as you will have more clarity, and a sense of what industry segments and roles within that segment will be a fit for your long term success.

Too many young professionals that are poised to enter into the sports industry do not really focus on this basic yet powerful initial assessment. It is very easy to convince yourself that you really like sales and you want to be selling season tickets for your favorite team or college sports program. You tell yourself, "I am outgoing, I like talking with people." But you quickly learn that it takes more than just a good outgoing personality to be a successful salesperson.

There are sales quotas; there is a great deal of pressure to close more and more sales each and every day/week/month. For some, that type of inherent pressure takes the joy out of what they are doing. Conversely, sales are a great opportunity to break into the sports industry, as by sheer attrition there are always sales openings. Nothing happens in sports, no ad revenue, no parking revenue, no concession revenue, no luxury suite revenue, nothing, until the turnstiles are moving.

If you can stomach some of the inherent challenges and bring results, you are more likely to move within the company into other areas of the front office. (By the way, I have seen many people take on a sales role and make a very good living!) I have seen it time and again, that someone who has a good track record of success in sales is a highly desired candidate for other roles.

A key example of another assessment is to create a list of your true interests, which match your top assets (skills) and then create a list of target companies who are in that line of work and then target contacts within those companies.

I recently worked with a young woman who had a successful athletic career in both college softball and volleyball. She tried her hand in coaching those sports but it did not fulfill her. In talking with her I asked a few basic questions which promoted a nice spirited discussion about other options in and around her passions. Using softball as the example I mentioned all the equipment that is used for practice and for games and told her that there are companies such as Easton, Rawlings, Mizuno and Wilson (bats, gloves and shoes) to manufacturers of uniforms, hats, helmets, practice jerseys, game jerseys, balls, batting cages, batting gloves, score cards, instructional DVD's, specialized equipment that are used for drills just to name a few. I shared that each one of those companies manufacturing equipment has sales reps, marketing reps, trade show reps, special event planners and many other integral roles.

The point is, there are so many additional options in any given category within the sports industry to look into--that will offer a great opening to break in.

Another important facet to consider; look very carefully at what type of culture a potential company exhibits and operates under. There are methods to dig deeper into this other than just asking the question about the company culture during the interview process. Search on other websites, research the company name to read reviews, search who they do business with and make phone calls into some of their clients or partners to find out more about them. Most people will be willing to share with you what it is like to do business with them as long as you are clear that you are being considered for employment and want to learn as much as possible about your future potential employer. Another option is to leverage LinkedIn to learn more, from others who do not work there, to get their perspective on the company's reputation in terms of how they treat their employees, partners and customers and what type of company culture they offer.

Within LinkedIn alone you can search the company and research former employees, and these are the people I would target to get their opinion. This can be an often over-looked element in the job search process but in my opinion, it is a very important ingredient for long-term success. If a company's culture appears to be a nice fit with your own personal style and methodology, then you are in a better position to make a solid decision if and when an offer is presented. When it comes to self-assessments or even taking inventory of your skills, the one main question I always lead with is this:

"What is your one main asset right now?" For me, it has always been the interpersonal communications skill set. For others it might be your technical skill set, your writing skill, your video editing skill, your web design skill, your social media skill, etc. Take note of your one main asset and leverage it, build on it and play to your strength.

HALFTIME!
Memorable Career Moments

As you develop trust and relationships, you will have opportunities to take photographs with prominent people in professional sports. These photos can be helpful for self-promotion when you want to continue to grow in the profession and at times a picture is worth more than a 1000 words!

Jerry Rice- Simply put, to me, JR is the greatest of all time. I first met Jerry back in 1991 during my intern year with the 49ers but it wasn't until he retired that I asked him to join me for the photo. He couldn't have been any nicer and when JR shook my hand, his hands are so big that his fingers went up to my forearm.

Joe Starkey, the long time radio voice of the 49ers. This picture was taken before his last game of a 20 year career announcing the 49ers. Joe will always be remembered for his historic call of the Cal vs. Stanford Big Game in 1982. Joe is still the radio voice of the University of California football, a role he has had since 1975.

When the opportunity presented itself to work with two NFL legends, it did not take long to accept the challenge. **Sonny Jurgensen** and **Sam Huff**, two Hall of Fame players that are the radio broadcast team for Washington Redskins Radio. This shot was before a game in 2006. Both players who were known to be true characters of the game did not disappoint! They shared wonderful stories during the broadcast and taught me that it is possible have fun while working a demanding role.

Jon Gruden / Ron Jaworski- Matt with the crew from Monday Night Football at Candlestick Park in 2010. Gruden is a no nonsense football guy but still nice enough to take this picture with me. I always find it interesting to meet and work with people that I used to admire from afar. To meet Gruden, the successful head coach was unique. I liked him as the coach of the Raiders and felt a sense of loss when he left for Tampa Bay. Jaworski is a former All Pro QB and one of the nicest guys in broadcast sports. The funny thing about my encounter with "Jaws" is that as a fan in 1980, I rooted against him when his Eagles faced the Raiders in SuperBowl XV. The lesson I learned is that he is so much more than #7 for the Eagles! A very good guy to work with.

Franco Harris / Paul Horung - This picture was taken as part of the celebration of the 75th anniversary of the NFL. Hornung along with, O.J Simpson and Earl Campbell are the only people to have won the Heisman Trophy, been selected as first overall National Football League draft picks, and been inducted into the Pro Football Hall of Fame. Franco Harris, the legendary running back from the Pittsburgh Steelers. Just like Jaworski, Franco was a guy I didn't root for as a player but he won me over by being a true gentleman.

Tom Flores, Flores was the NFL's first minority head coach to win a Super Bowl, winning twice - Super Bowl XV with the Oakland Raiders and Super Bowl XVIII with the Los Angeles Raiders, the latter victory being the only such in the history of NFL football in Southern California.

Flores also holds a rare distinction: Winning a Super Bowl both as a player (KC Chiefs) and as a coach (Raiders). This picture was taken prior to a Raiders vs. 49ers game in 2009.

Warren Moon- In 2009, I got the chance to work with Hall of Famer Warren Moon. This shot was taken before he entered the broadcast booth to announce for his team, the Seattle Seahawks. Warren was very calm, relaxed and has an air of quiet confidence about him. I've had the great luxury of meeting a lot of Hall of Famers and Warren is up there in terms of former players I was excited to meet.

Eddie Debartolo- As long as I've been associated with the 49ers, the chance to get a snapshot with the legendary former 49ers owner was too good to pass up. During his twenty-three years owning the team, beginning in 1977, the 49ers won an unprecedented five Super Bowls under coaches Bill Walsh and George Seifert, Super Bowl XVI, Super Bowl XIX, Super Bowl XXIII, Super Bowl XXIV, and Super Bowl XXIX. From the early 1980s through the 1990s, DeBartolo presided over a team that had the "winningest" decade in football history. "Mr. D" couldn't have been any more pleasant, taking the time to have a long conversation during the pre-game activities in 2011.

John Robinson- One of the all time great college coaches while at USC, Robinson also coached in the NFL with the Los Angeles Rams. Robinson's USC teams won four Rose Bowls and captured a share of the national championship in the 1978 season. I used to have a running inside joke about him with my brother and my dad but when the opportunity presented itelf to work with him on a radio broadcast, I was not joking anymore. A good guy who sure knows how to share some funny stories.

This picture of **Steve Young** and I was taken after a Monday Night Football Game in 2010. After his Hall of Fame career, Steve has turned out to be one the best TV analysts. Steve's personal story of being ready for his opportunity when it presented itself is epic. His journey to stardom was not an easy one and anyone can learn from how he handled the adversity. A truly inspiring athlete and person.

3rd Quarter
The 4 P Coaching Model

How to Effectively Manage Your Career Search Process

You have more than likely heard the phrase, "to manage your career search it takes the same commitment, intensity and drive as if the search were a job itself." This is very true. You need to manage the job search process and break down each day's worth of activities as if it were a day on the job. Equally, if not more important, is the managing of your personal brand. You truly need to create a new mind-shift and become the Chief Marketing Officer of your own brand. No one will manage, protect and maintain a positive brand better than yourself. Nothing will happen in your career search unless your brand is marketed and displayed in the best possible manner.

This does not simply mean your Facebook page and Twitter feed should be closely guarded and protected like a bar of gold, it means it should be a top priority. Too often I see many of my coaching clients who fail to realize the importance of how social media can be a damaging element of a career search. We all enjoy Facebook, we all enjoy reading others' witty and seemingly harmless posts and posting our own status updates but we simply need to be mindful of the negative impacts of what a potential employer might see as an immediate red flag. Inappropriate pictures, updates or comments are public. Anyone can see them and many if not most hiring managers will make it a point to research a candidates background on Facebook as part of their due diligence.

What is The 4 P Coaching Model?

When I took a work hiatus a few years ago to clear my head, organize my thoughts and start to create my coaching model, the process was actually easier than I originally thought it would be. Why? I simply recalled the many learning moments I had during my 18 years in Corporate America.

Working for such firms as Microsoft and FedEx, I was privy to an impressive group of thought leaders, management teams, as well as some very smart colleagues and world class training sessions over the years. I consider myself to be a keen observer of people in general, and specifically life in the work place. Any role within a corporate structure can provide fabulous insight into the inner workings of how individuals, groups and teams operate.

 Just like in sports, some are truly special leaders who have the "it" factor of being a solid leader with charisma and a skill set to create a framework others willingly follow. While others have specialized skills, be they in marketing, sales, IT, administrative or support roles. All are equally as important and have a large impact on the success any team will achieve. I have been witness to and collaborated with just about all of these roles in some way, shape, or fashion and have learned some valuable lessons not only from strategic management but peers and support teams. I simply took the best of the best lessons I've learned, some the hard way and some through success on the job, and created a simple, easy to understand and most important, easy to implement four step coaching process.

Over the years I have taken part in numerous marketing seminars, strategic selling training sessions, executive leadership forums, effective public speaking workshops and a variety of sales methodology courses. Most were good but took far too long to get to the heart of the content and hence lost the attendee's attention. For this reason alone, when I was creating my coaching model, I knew I wanted it to be easy to absorb, easy to follow, and for it to be direct and to the point.

When I was reviewing my notes as part of my creation process, it became very clear what the focal points were going to be. It just so happened that each category was a word that started with the letter P. Perfect, I'll call it my 4 P coaching process.

- ***Position***
- ***Promotion***
- ***Package***
- ***Partnerships***

Position:

The key to the 4 P coaching model is that is goes in sequential order and for a reason. To start; no career search process can take shape unless you have a finely tuned statement of purpose. In other words, how do you plan on **positioning** yourself to the target market(s) you are going after? This first step is going to be used in both written form as well as verbal. *(Verbal is a big key as you will need to clearly articulate your positioning* *statement in many face to face meetings or on phone calls).* Many of my coaching clients do not yet have a specific target industry segment they want to go after and when that is the case, I guide them through a series basic and advanced questions and assessments to help create a more defined road map they can work from.

I always make it really clear to my clients, it is OK to not have a clear picture of what you want to do, however, it is important to continue to make strides in creating and refining your personal career search road map.

As much as I enjoy working with my clients on all phases of the 4 P process, the first step always brings out that "a-ha" moment, which is a great feeling for me and more importantly for my clients. Some keys to consider when crafting your first positioning statement include--do not aim for perfection. Just start by drafting a few sentences at a minimum to two paragraphs at a maximum; extracting a few key points from your background (resume) and how you plan on leveraging your practical experiences into a new role.

Here is an example of a positioning statement from a client who is looking to break into the event planning/event management segment of the sports industry.

Dating back to my high school years, I was part of the committee that planned and executed a series of successful youth sports camps. Now at the University of_____, I am part of the game day event planning commission. With the great experiences I have had to date I am looking to leverage my practical knowledge into the _____ role (add job title you are applying for) and be a valued member of your team.

Here are a few additional guidelines that will help you craft a compelling positioning statement.

1. Define your intention. What do you want to happen as a result of your two to three-minute elevator positioning statement? Remember, your goal is to "advance the ball," not score a touchdown.

2. Examine your scenario. Is this talk for a planned or a spontaneous situation? Preparing accordingly can help you earn the right to be heard.

3. Draft your basic positioning statement. Think about your message, your goals, your creative ideas and your persuasive arguments. Structure must be paired with progression. Your listeners want to know that you're heading somewhere as you build up to your conclusion and your close.

4. Build your case. Explain to listeners why they need you, and your skill set; why they should hire you. Provide valid reasons and proof so your arguments pass the "So what?" test.

5. Don't forget to close. (a.k.a CALL TO ACTION) Present your prospect with a clear directive and a respectful call to action. Ask for that next appointment, follow-up call or meeting. Make it easy and painless for the listener to take the next step with you.

6. Get creative. Do your homework on your audience or prospects, crafting an approach that speaks directly to their needs. Ramp up your creative nature and customize your talk to intrigue your prospects; give them a reason to want to meet with you again.

7. Speak in your own voice. Try a conversational approach that allows you to be comfortable and true to yourself and your personality. Communicate your experience, vision and excitement directly—in a way that only you can.

8. Write it out. Write out the long version and recite it. Then transfer your core statement of purpose and key points and phrases to an index card.

9. Practice, practice, practice. Review your positioning statement again and again until it feels like a natural part of your everyday communication.

10. Use it! Any positioning statement is only effective if you use it!

Promotion:

The key question to ask yourself as you plan your career search strategy is this, "What is your plan to effectively promote yourself, your brand and how do you plan to promote your positioning statement?" In today's "look at me" world of social media it is very challenging to strike the right balance of self-promotion and being humble. On one side there is the great quote from P.T. Barnum of Barnum and Bailey Circus fame:

"Something terrible happens without promotion—nothing!"

On the other hand, it is very important to be aware of the balance and not overdo your self-promotion. I referenced LinkedIn already and it is worth repeating. LinkedIn is such a valuable tool and it has the qualities of professionalism and integrity already built in. By posting updates about you and your career goals not only to your own profile but also on the industry groups function, it will help you immensely. Finding the right balance is the key. Too much self-promotion will turn people off. Too little and no one will know who you are or what you are looking to accomplish.

Reaching out to your direct contacts first is always a good first approach. Make sure to also reach out to your second tier contacts, those that still know you, but will also provide you with realistic feedback. My clients appreciate the fact that I am a sounding board for them and more importantly a resource that will not tell them what they want to hear. As their career coach, I am someone who will be their "reality check." I'm not harsh but at the same time I provide a realistic support system. The point here is this:

Be sure to reach out to others in your inner circle, not just those that will agree with everything you say. You need to be stretched and held accountable in a way that will help you grow professionally and force you to look at your career search in ways that are tough to do on your own.

Package:

This particular "P" brings about the biggest mind-shift in my clients. They ask, "What do you mean by package myself to any given employer?"

The right packaging of your message (Positioning) and your story (Promotion) needs to support your goal(s). You should treat your job search process as if you are the CMO, Chief Marketing Officer, of your own brand. After all, who is going to promote, market and brand yourself with as much power and professionalism than you?

What exactly is branding yourself?

In today's market there are many ways to create and maintain a good brand. To have your own website or blog where people can see or read what you do is one way. If you are in broadcast, have your physical demo reel ready, and the same applies if you are in graphic design; have your portfolio nicely packaged in a folder, with your business card.

I always coach my clients, regardless of what segment they are pursuing within the sports industry, to have a handful of nice folders from an office supply store and place your resume, statement of purpose on one side and some key testimonials on the other. Testimonials carry more weight because they are written statements about you, the kind of work you have done and the type of work style you have. Ask anyone you have worked for, volunteered for or reported to, to write one for you. Add a business card and there you have it! These days there are many online suppliers who virtually give business card orders away, hoping for your repeat business and loyalty. A nice little leave behind is a folder for those that you meet or interview with.

In today's click and send world, a folder of information is a nice touch. In the event you have a phone meeting, send your folder via USPS or UPS / FedEx if you have the extra money and mail it off in advance if possible. I can tell you this, regular mail is refreshing as everyone relies on email. To receive a envelope is a novelty. It also shows you have taken the time to package yourself with care.

So are you really a brand?

YES YOU ARE.

I like to use the supermarket analogy. When you go to your local market and shop for the staples like bread, shampoo, cereal, etc...you have a pretty good reason for the products you buy, right? It could be the price, could be the fact it is something your parents used to buy for you, could be that your favorite celebrity endorses it, or you like the colors of the logo; and there are a few other reasons I'm sure. What prompts you to buy a product?

The fact is, there is some compelling reason you bought the product on the shelf versus buying the many other competing products that are on the same shelf. Apply this scenario to you, as the CMO of your own brand, and think about how you can brand and package yourself to an employer that will give them reason to buy you (hire you). Be mindful of your brand, protect it and market it with the highest level of integrity and professionalism possible. Take a hard look at how you can create a leave behind folder that will give a manager good cause to look at you as the person they hire.

Partnerships:

The main goal of partnerships is to form a small group or advisory board that will grow over time, that can help you. The people you partner and collaborate with that can help get your message out is key. For some, their advisory board may already be in place without even knowing it. Immediate family, boyfriends and girlfriends, rabbis or pastors, college professors, career coaches, you get the idea.

After this initial board of advisors is in place you can reach out and extend yourself to others that are willing to help out.

This is where I come in. As shameless a plug as this may be, it is true. All of the above mentioned contacts are great but they will more than likely only tell you what you want to hear not what you need to hear. There is a very big difference! Of course we all need to build up our confidence but at some point you are better served to have a balanced sounding board.

You'll grow to appreciate a safe resource you can count on to help guide you and provide honest and critical feedback. This will help your ideas grow, it will help you grow your brand, and it will help expand your horizons.

Finding a business mentor is not that easy and usually happens without even knowing it. It just takes shape over time and there is nothing wrong with gong back to the contacts you have formed and asking for advice from those you connected with early on.

Those already in the industry, with good experience and tenure generally like to help by giving back. I know I do and that is the main reason I am a career coach.

5th P just for added measure- Persistence:

It almost goes without saying but being persistent is a good quality, when persistence is used correctly. No one likes the feeling of being hounded or receiving multiple emails or phone calls each day, so be mindful of this. Spacing out your phone calls or emails over the course of a few weeks or a month might turn out to be a better approach.

Finding the right balance of sticking with it and being the squeaky wheel is a challenge for most, just use yourself as the benchmark. Would you want someone calling you three times a day? Probably not.

There is nothing wrong with sending a US Mail letter to someone you are trying to reach. It is a refreshing approach that will bring you results so consider adding this technique to your bag of tricks! For me personally, there have been many occasions where I was diligent in my follow up, spaced my connections out over a period of time, leveraged emails and phone calls with US Mail letters and never heard back.

There does come a time when even the most professional and tactful persistence fails to bring results. Move on. It is counterintuitive but at the same time you will be spending your time more wisely and can refocus on making other connections.

4 C's to keep in mind.

I have talked about it before but want to detail the 4 C's of effective communication.

Be **Clear**

In today's world, attention spans are short. Make good use of the face time you get as well as the phone time. Don't rush your message and just do a data dump of your story during your meetings but be aware that you should get to your key points in a timely and natural manner and be sure to keep it conversational.

Be **Concise**

Often times this is confused or blended together with being clear. Be concise with your messaging and pay particular attention to any given key points you are delivering and make sure you do not carry on too long.

Be **Confident**

There is a big difference in being confident and being arrogant. I have seen both and any hiring manager that has some experience will recognize the difference right away. Confidence comes in a few forms such as your body language, the way you make eye contact and the way you deliver your message with purpose. Act like you have been in the scenario before and it will help you immensely.

Call to Action

Too many times I have been in meetings and the person I am meeting with will ace all facets of the meeting but forget to end with a call to action.

If you are in a relaxed networking meeting, ask if you can stay in touch. You also now have the right to ask your contact if there is anyone they can suggest you get in touch with that may help you broaden your network. (This step is overlooked far too much) If your contact accepted your meeting in the first place, you have the right at the end of that meeting to ask them if they would be willing to review their personal connections to see if they have anyone that would make sense for you to reach out to. By the way, always ask for permission to use their name. If you are in a formal interview, ask what the steps are in the interviewing process for the company. Make sure you express your interest in the role too! That is always a nice call to action! The goal is to always keep the dialog going, to keep it moving forward.

Overtime

Networking- it is such a buzzword in the business world but such an important facet of your ongoing development that I would like to share a few simple but critical steps to networking and relationship building.

It is easy to get caught up in building a growing network, which is fine if that's your goal. I always advise to be strategic in your networking efforts. Instead of trying to build up a large number of contacts, start small and focus on connecting with people that can really create a difference for you. Above all, be mindful and send occasional follow-ups to them on your progress. By going this route you will build a solid foundation and also create a small inner circle that will eventually become your very own advisory board.

You should never stop networking but be sure to be mindful when you are reaching out to people. Be clear, honest and appreciative of their willingness to assist you. Always strive to connect and stay connected with those that you can learn from and be sure to pay it back when the time is right!

Never forget that solid, effective networking is always built on trust and reciprocity. If you understand and value both, there's no end to the growth of your network and career. Vigorously build and track your network.

Networking is smart business – build your network before you need it.

Protect your networking connectors and appreciate your networking advocates.

Be completely familiar with your own skills and talents.

Remember: Benefits Always Trump Features. You need to give people motivation if you want them to help you. You need to sell your benefits.

The combination of a top-notch positioning statement and extraordinary networking will get you to your desired career goals.

I was asked during a radio interview recently to share a few things I wish I knew back when I first started out in the business world. Things that maybe could have made my journey easier or lessons I wish weren't so hard learned. It got me thinking about where I've been, what I've jumped over and the roadmap I wish someone had handed me when I was still fresh-eyed and new to the business world.

I wanted to expand on some of the answers I gave during that interview. Below are some key line items no one told me about business—that I really wish they would have.

1. You can save yourself 10 redundant emails (and maybe some hurt feelings) simply by picking up the phone or walking across the room to ask the person that question you're trying to type out in an email.

2. There will be days when you really don't want to get out of bed to start up again. Do it anyway. Unless there are tears involved. Then stay there until you can make them stop.

3. When in management: Firing people sucks, but employing people who don't fit sucks even harder. Look for culture and value fit. Most other things can be taught, picked up, or tactfully coached into people.

4. Regardless of what level you have attained, you'll learn more from people who think differently than you, than from those who share your way of thinking. My greatest business conversations have been with people who sit on the opposite side of the spectrum from me. They may have differing thoughts than me but they have the ability to voice them in a professional manner.

5. Today's nemesis may be tomorrow's ally. The opposite is also true.

6. If something's not working, change it. It is a key leadership metric to recognize that you must fail faster, and move on quickly.

7. Today's hot trends are tomorrow's Pinterest. Focus on what you're after, not the tool you're using today to get there. Twitter may not last, but your need to have real-time conversations with colleagues as well as customers and approach them on their terms will remain. How will you do it post-Twitter?

8. If you're lucky, your employees, interns or colleagues will always be smarter than you. Embrace that and never stop learning.

9. You will become whom you align yourself with. Pick wisely. (Be strategic when networking.)

10. If possible, always take the coffee or lunch meeting. You never know where it will lead or what unlikely friendship it will create. That stranger in the bar could grow up to be your business partner.

11. No is a complete sentence. Be nice about it though!

12. Hire an accountant; never touch your own books. That's not your strong suit and it's a waste of your time to mess it up.

13. Getting involved with Internet drama, public flame wars or emotional train wrecks are for people with too much time on their hands. It's distracting and will derail you from your real purpose.

14. Always remember why you're doing this. Know, at your core, what you're trying to build and why you're trying to build it. It will see you out of some difficult times. Make sure your team remembers it, too.

15. Don't trust people who routinely answer questions you never asked. They're trying to justify something – maybe to you, maybe to themselves. Either way, it probably won't help you.

16. Having people write disparaging blog posts with your name in the title is a sign you're doing something right. Your skin will get thicker and it will be okay. You'll actually come to find the attacks amusing.

17. You won't always know what you're doing or have all the answers. You just need to know where to go to find them. Or at least have the backbone to make a decision and stick with it.

18. When debating with someone, act under the assumption that you're right. Even if you're not. If you show uncertainty, you lose anyway.

19. The world will not end if you don't get that blog post out on time. Eat dinner. And go for that run.

20. The best clients are the ones you'd be friends with and who you'd happily support even if they weren't paying you.

21. If the client isn't happy, it's probably because you did a poor job establishing expectations. Make every attempt to do it better next time.

22. You'll get more from promoting others than you will from promoting yourself. You'll also learn more, be introduced to cooler people, and hear about things sooner.

23. Business is based around relationships. The relationship you have with your business partner, with your employees, with your colleagues, and especially with your competitors. Invest in them and cherish them. You're lucky to be surrounded by people constantly surprising you.

24. Talent and luck only get you so far. You need to create your own opportunity.

25. Think before you execute, but don't get stuck there. A mediocre idea that's acted upon will always trump the genius idea still in your head.

26. You are going to meet some amazing people. You just have to relax enough to enjoy the ride.

I wish someone had sat me down and told me these 26 things when I started on this path and I wanted to share them with you in hopes some of them may help you along your journey. These by no means are the golden rules, simply some select lessons I've learned along the way

What is your inner voice telling you? Will you prepared for success? What role will you play in the sports industry? Will you be ready when it's your time to **get in the game?**

4th Quarter
Special Guest Contributions

With my many years in the sports industry I thought it would make sense to create a "snapshot" of real world advice from others who have roles that make the sports business happen. I have included a select few personal contacts of mine from various sports industry segments, to provide a sneak peek on their career evolution. The goal with these contributions is to provide some additional advice and guidance from others as well as my own.

DUKE BOBBER- Internet coordinator for all the web properties of the Green Bay Packers (NFL)

Q-How did you creatively present or package yourself to land the role you are currently in? **(interview strategies)**

A- The most important thing to remember is that in an interview setting, you're there to sell yourself. I knew I wanted to set myself apart from the rest of the pack, so it was crucial to present myself in the most professional manner possible. The cover letter, in my case, is the first glimpse a potential employer has into your potential. I think it's easy to fall into the trap of using clichés like "hard working" and "a real go-getter." I tried to give some insight into where I've been in my career and where I aspire to be. Injecting personality into the cover letter is something that I don't think a lot of job-seekers do enough of. I also spent a great deal of time putting together a portfolio of the work I was most proud of. Anything you can hand your potential employer is another potential reason for them to hire you. The biggest challenge is setting yourself apart.

LOU IMBRIANO-

Lou Imbriano, the Vice President and Chief Marketing Officer of the New England Patriots football team from 1997-2006, is President and CEO of TrinityOne, a marketing company specializing in creating strategy for corporations to maximize revenue generation through building customer relationships and custodians of the brand. Lou, who teaches sports marketing at Boston College, is based in Boston, MA and is the author *Winning the Customer,* from McGraw-Hill. Lou can be found at LouImbriano.com

How Hard Can It Be?

When I began my career in radio, I worked on the creative, rather than the business side of the industry. I was in the programming department and would write and produce for different shows. I would devour the newspapers every day looking for potential topics and comedy bits. It was fun, and my mind was thinking very differently from my later focus on how to build relationships and generate revenue. Although, I was still practicing the relationship aspect when booking guests for the show.

I was fortunate to take to both the job and the industry, and I was promoted along the way within programming. However, at some point, I realized that I was working at the only sports radio station in Boston; I never wanted to leave Boston, but I thought that there had to be more for me for a career. At the time of this epiphany, the station manager was also running marketing – her name was Bev Tilden. Bev had a very creative radio mind and she understood how to get listeners to tune in and stay tuned. As always in radio, one GM left and another came in and Bev just didn't click with the new GM. So, Bev was off to another challenge.

The GM came to me and said, "Lou, Bev is moving on. We love what you're doing in programming, so you're fine, but we will need to search for a new marketing director." I had a moment of clarity. It was like you'd see on a TV show where everything stops around you, but you are still moving at full speed. In an all-out, overachiever, knee-jerk response I said, "Let me do it." The new GM, John Maguire, gave me a smirk and said, "Lou, you're great at programming but what do you know about marketing?" This was when I adopted my mantra that I still utter today when questioned or challenged: "How hard can it be?"

John chuckled and said that the station needed someone with marketing experience, because it had the potential to become #1 in the ratings. Again, with more balls than brains, I pushed on. I asked, "How long will it take you to find a new marketing director?" He pondered and stated that it would be three months or so, which led me to a life changing moment. I said to him, "Let me do it while you are searching so we don't lose any ground. You don't have to pay me anything extra, and if I'm slacking in my primary function, you say the word and I will focus purely on programming." I'm paraphrasing, of course, because that was almost 20 years ago – but that was the general conversation.

I guess I made a valid pitch because he agreed. Once I got a hold of the opportunity I wasn't letting go.

Three months turned into a couple of years, and this inexperienced, untrained marketing director was over-achieving and delivering beyond expectations. I'd never had a marketing job; I'd never taken a marketing class. Yet I was marketing this sports station onto the map. The funny thing was that at one point after achieving some marketing success, I remember giving a programming concept to an on-air talent, and he said to me, "Lou, you're great at marketing, but leave the programming to us." Ha, I'd remade myself so much that I was now viewed not as a programming person with six years experience, but as a marketing guy.

And there was no looking back. Because I had no preconceived notion on how to market, it allowed me to be open to and create different ways to engage with our consumers – listeners. The key to all of this was that I understood the programming of the station better than most. Because I was creating programming to engage and entertain the listeners, I had to know who the listeners were and what they liked. I was in-tune with our listeners and I knew how to interest them so they would check us out. I knew how reach our listeners because I talked with and listened to them.

Later, when given the opportunity to run marketing for the New England Patriots, I stuck to my mantra of, "How hard can it be?" And again, when asked to teach a marketing class at Boston College – "How hard can it be?" If you get nothing else from this post, never let anyone tell you that it can't be done or that you are not qualified. You can do anything if you truly want to. And please note, if I can do it, anyone can. Besides, "How hard can it be?"

MIKE HACKMAN- Basketball Sports Marketng, Nike, Inc

Q- What event or series of events were paramount to you breaking into the sports industry?

A- I went to graduate school to get a master's degree in sports marketing. As part of that degree, I was able to get an internship at the Indiana Sports Corporation where I was hired full time at the end of the internship.

Q -How did you creatively present or package yourself to land the role you are currently in. **(interview strategies)**

A- I wasn't overly creative. I was hired by Nike from the Indiana Sports Corporation because they were impressed with my work managing the Nike account. I demonstrated my value by doing my job the best I could and they noticed me. All employers are looking for people who can add value to what they do. My best advice is to demonstrate there is no one more valuable to achieving their organization's goals than you.

Q -How would you guide someone in today's market to find the balance of differentiating themselves from other candidates without overdoing it?

A- I think that will always be a hit or miss proposition. You should always convey your passion, but the risk of appearing fake or comical is always there. My advice would be to find out as much as possible about the people conducting the interview and tailor your message to them. When all else fails, trust your gut. You've gotta be you and you'll be better off in the long run finding a role that fits --than faking an interview to just to get a job.

Q -What three or four career search strategies would you advise someone to utilize in today's employment market.

A- I really believe your career will find you if you stay true to yourself and do something you are passionate about. If you wake up and don't want to go to work, then you should find something else. Do what you enjoy and keep your eyes open for opportunities. Once you figure out what you really want your career to be then develop a plan for where you want to go.

Q - Please detail an effective method/technique that someone recently displayed in networking with you.

A- The best way to really network with people is to help them first. If you genuinely serve others without an agenda, you'll be repaid over and over.

Q- Please detail an effective strategy/technique someone utilized on you during an interview process.

A- The most effective strategy I've seen is when a guy came in with an entire portfolio that detailed our industry, our target audience, our strategies and his experience and specific abilities that would add value to our department. The amount of work that went into it alone was impressive.

Q- What advice or guidance was given to you from a mentor that you would be willing to share?

A- There are three things to never fear – change, failure and surrounding yourself with people smarter than you are.

ERIN OBRIEN- Vice President of Ruff Neck Scarves

Q -What event or series of events were paramount to you breaking into the sports industry?

A- For us we had a competitor that we tried to work with that had, and still has, bad customer service. We thought an opportunity existed to sell the same product but provide fantastic customer service. Many events took place to help establish our company but I think flexibility has been critical. Changing rapidly with the market has helped us a lot.

Q -How would you guide someone in today's market to find the balance of differentiating themselves from other candidates w/out overdoing it?

A- Show that you have passion for the business as well as for the game. Try to learn about the business regardless of whether or not you will land an interview or a job.

Q - What three or four career search strategies would you advise someone to utilize in today's employment market.

A- Networking is critical through social media such as Twitter and LinkedIn – plus professional groups and events such as trade shows. Also don't be afraid to pick up the phone and call the person.

Q - Please detail an effective method/technique that someone recently displayed in networking with you.

A- Asking me through LinkedIn if they can buy me coffee to discuss our company and letting me pick the time and place. They also offered to help for free if needed.

Q -Please detail an effective strategy/technique someone utilized on you during an interview process.

A- Always shoot for that balance of not only presenting your skills and background, but asking well thought out questions. Show you've done your homework.

Q -What advice or guidance was given to you from a mentor that you would be willing to share?

A- Do what you love so that you don't feel miserable going to work. You have to believe in what you are doing.
http://www.ruffneckscarves.com/

ANDY DOLICH - Veteran Sports Executive with the rare distinction of holding C-level positions in all four major sports

<u>*SO YOU WANT TO WORK IN SPORTS?*</u>

You say you want one of the 60,000 sports jobs that are out there. Well genius, how are you going to get one when the take-a-number machine is at 495,000 and climbing? This alarming stat comes from Teamwork Consulting, one of the country's leading executive recruiting firms in the sports industry.

Having spent 39 years in the front offices of teams in the NBA (National Basketball League), NFL (National Football League), NHL (National Hockey League), MLB (Major League Baseball), NASL (North American Soccer League), NLL (National Lacrosse League), three years as the owner of my own sports consulting business, and two years with tickets.com, there are a number of simple steps that, when followed, will greatly improve any new job seeker's chances of getting their high priced athletic footwear in the door.

Step 1.) **Take the billionaire litmus test**

This one is easy. Just check your bank account. Does it have 10 digits? If yes, go on to Step 2, purchase a major league sports franchise. Depending on the team, they can go from a strip mall like $80 million to a Rodeo Drive excessive $1.2 billion. Step 3 is easy. Buy the team and install yourself, the spouse, your kids, their friends, close relatives and your favorite pets in any front office position you choose. If you don't qualify in Step 1, then skip to Step 4 which is going about the job search the old fashioned way, by "earning it."

Step 4.) **Sports Management Programs –**

There you are wasting your parents' or your own hard earned cash at some institution of higher learning. Are you having fun majoring in something that you have no intention of ever using at any time during your time on earth? Be truthful, you are spending more time watching SportsCenter and hanging out at the student union eyeballing the talent or betting on your alma mater's games than you are logging time in the library, lab or actually going to class.

In the early 1950's, Walter O'Malley, the owner of the Brooklyn Dodgers, saw the future and it was sports management. He helped fund the first program at Columbia University in New York City headed by Dr. Clifford Brownell and his associate Dr. James Mason. The program never got off the ground.

When the Dodgers moved west, Mason took the program lock stock and barrel and re-kindled O'Malley's brainchild at Ohio University in Athens. Ohio University has matured into the Harvard of Sports Management Programs with over 1,500 graduates holding key management positions throughout the sports industry.

Ohio University: www.cats.ohiou.edu/sportsadmin

Today in the U.S., there are over 320 sports management programs offered at the undergrad and graduate level. Visit some of these programs in person or online to get an idea of what they have to offer.

Other significant national programs are:

University of Oregon (Warsaw Sports Management): www.warsawcenter.com

University of Massachusetts at Amherst: http://www.isenberg.umass.edu/sportmgt/

University of Central Florida (Devos Sports Management): http://web.bus.ucf.edu/sportbusiness/

University of Memphis: http://coe.memphis.edu/hss/

University of San Francisco: http://www.usfca.edu/artsci/grad/sport_management/index.html

New York University: http://www.scps.nyu.edu/areas-of-study/tisch/undergraduate-programs/bs-in-sports-management/

Robert Morris College: http://www.rmu.edu/web/cms/schools/sbus/sport-management/Pages/ug-sport-mgmnt.aspx

University of Tennessee: http://web.utk.edu/~sals/ug/Sport.html

West Virginia University: http://www.wvu.edu/~physed/sportman.htm

Ohio State University: www.coe.ohio-state.edu

Mt. Union College: https://www.muc.edu/academics/academic_ programs/sport_management

Northwestern University: www.scs.northwestern.edu/grad/ sports

Columbia University: www.ce.columbia.edu/sports13
SUNY Cortland: www.Cortland.edu/SPMG

50 years after the fact, Columbia has started a program. The greatest change in the past 10 years has been the maturation of these programs into MBA programs. Most of the early programs were undergrad.

These programs won't necessarily give you all the right stuff, but they are the most impactful industry shoehorn that you can hope to have without your daddy's billions or some major inside hookup. All graduates of these programs are sought after by sports organizations for one simple reason: their students have proven interest in the business and they are the most affordable highly educated inventory in today's job market.

5.) **Letter writing -**

The lost art of communication through the printed word on a piece of real paper. Just because you send someone a cyber communication doesn't vault you to the front of the line. Junk mail is junk mail no matter how it is packaged and delivered. Think contrarian, when everyone is going one way, take the path less traveled. I will always respond to a well crafted letter that has my name and title correctly spelled and I can tell that the writer has spent more than a nanosecond doing some research about the team they are writing to. Never ask for a job in your letter and never talk about the time you played high school sports and how much sports TV you watch or read about. Victory is snagging an informational interview. The content of your letter should show what skills you have that would be beneficial to the organization. It is critically important that the letter is crafted in a way that it seems personal and not mass produced. Show your personality in the letter; think of it as an audition.

6.) **You are what you read -**

You had better work on educating yourself about the insularity of the industry. There aren't many publications and daily updates on what is happening in the sports business. In sports you will need to get a subscription to Sports Business Journal and Sports Business Daily, ESPN (the magazine), Wall Street Journal and USA Today, which will tell you on a daily and weekly basis what is happening in the sports biz.

You will need to connect the dots to figure out where and when to fish for a job based on the intelligence gathering you are doing. You need to know when a CEO is fired, when ownership changes, when there's a new team, a new league, a new RSN (regional sports network), or a new AD (Athletic Director).

Check all the teams' and leagues' websites for job openings, which come and go in the blink of an eye. Get yourself one of the industry information "bibles" that will list the names and addresses of every sports organization known to man:

INDUSTRY RESOURCE GUIDES:

Team Marketing Report - Sports Sponsor Factbook:
www.teammarketing.com

Sports Business Journal - Resource Guide & Factbook:
www.sportsbusinessjournal.com

National Sports Marketing Network:
www.sportsmarketingnetwork.com

Be sure to update your sources from season to season. Positions change as much as the weather.

Read to succeed – Sports Business Books:

Sports Inc - Phil Schaff

Veeck as in Wreck, 30 Tons a Day and The Hustler's Handbook - Bill Veeck

Sport Marketing - Mullin, Hardy & Sutton

The Dream Job: Sports Publicity, Promotion & Marketing - Mel Helitzer

The Business of Sports - Rosner & Shropshire

Ice to the Eskimos – Jim Spoelstra

Marketing Outrageously - Jim Spoelstra

Meaning of Sports - Mandelbaum

A Hard Road to Glory – Arthur Ashe

Forty Million Dollar Slaves – Rhoden

Moneyball – Michael Lewis

Ethics in Sport – Morton

Sport Promotion & Sales Management – Richard Irwin

Sports Business in the Global Marketplace – Westerbeek

7.) Work like a jerk -

So the competition is disgustingly bright. Remember those several hundred thousand other job seekers? What chance do you have when the first time job seeker has an undergraduate degree from Stanford, just got their law degree from Harvard and is on the Nobel Prize waiting list? It does not mean that the school you went to or the grades you had will be the ultimate determining factor. It is simple; just make sure that you outwork anyone associated with the organization.

If the office hours are 9 to 5, you are there early and the last to leave. There isn't a request that you don't say yes to unless it is talking investment strategy with Bernie Madoff.

You will be amazed at how many opportunities show up before an office opens and after most everyone has left for the day. You will be answering the phone and more often than not it is the owner or some other bigwig calling early or late.

I met the legendary Lamar Hunt in my first week with the Philadelphia 76ers when he came into our office looking for a phone. I was the only one in the office. I drove Red Auerbach to the airport and had 20 minutes of one on one with him right at the beginning of my time with the 76ers.

I spent a lot of time managing to walk around to see who was in the office when they didn't have to be, especially on weekends. It is much easier to have some quality face time with the execs

66

of the team when the phones and the distractions of the day are over. Hard work is still prized by many top decision makers.

8.) **Sports Conferences and Symposiums -**

There are a number of regional and national meetings open to job seekers devoted to the business of sport. It is a great way to rub shoulders with prospective employers. The fees to participate are between $250 and $2,000 bucks.

Major opportunities are:

- The National Sports Forum: http://sports-forum.com/
- World Congress of Sports: http://www.sportsbusinessconferences.com/world-congress-of-sports/
- Sports Executive Leadership Conference - by invitation only
- Pro Sports Leagues Job Seekers sessions - check websites
- Sports Business Journal's specific sport symposiums
- Sports Careers Conference: www.sportscareers.com

9.) **Know when and where to fish**

Logic has never been a surplus for the job seekers who make up the herd. The largest volume of job inquiries usually comes to teams at the start of the season. Well, that's about six months too late. Use your brain. You want to get on the job runway at the end of the team's season when people are switching jobs, getting promoted or canned.

Unless you are a personal friend of the owner, don't write them a letter. Find out what is available and who is making the hiring decision. These days almost all teams list job opportunities on their team websites. Make sure you submit your electronic résumé to the team's HR Department.

10.) **It's the numbers stupid!**

The first question I ask job seekers during interviews is what they dream about as it relates to jobs. If they could wave a magic wand what would happen. Invariably the answer is that they want to be President or CEO of the team. My answer is, "Nice, but I'm President and have a multi-year contract." Then they go, "Oh I get it, I want to work for your team." They still don't get it. That means there are 100 jobs that you could apply for. "Oh I want to work for your league or one of the teams." Better, but still not the correct answer because there you have 3,000 jobs.

What you want to look at is the total universe of sports jobs - pro, collegiate, amateur, corporate, broadcasters, publishers, manufacturers, etc. It is a lot easier to catch a tuna in the middle of a school than trying to hook one in the middle of the open ocean. It's the numbers stupid.

11.) **Executive Recruiters**

There are a number of executive recruiting firms that specialize in the world of sports business. As you start out on your job search, make sure you get your information on as many databases as you can. The #1 firm in the country is Teamwork Consulting which is headed by industry veteran Buffy Filippell. These firms and their principles are hired to do retained searches for all types of sports teams, organizations and associated entities. From time to time, the larger major international recruiting firms are selected to do searches for lead positions such as commissioner, CEO and President.

The top sports industry recruiting firms are:
- Teamwork Consulting – www.teamworkonline.com
- Eastman & Beaudine – www.eastman-beaudine.com

- James & Company – www.jamescosearch.com
- General Sports – www.generalsports.com
- Game Face Marketing – www.gamefaceinc.com
- Turnkey Sports – www.turnkeysports.com
- Sportsearch – www.sportsearch.net
- Korn Ferry – www.kornferry.com
- Spencer Stuart – www.spencerstuart.com
- Heidrick & Struggles - http://www.heidrick.com/default.aspx
- Russell Reynolds – www.russellreynolds.com
- Six Figure Sports – www.sixfiguresports.com

12.) **Yes and No – Do's and Don'ts**

These points can help you in your job search and the interview process:

<u>Yes / Do It!</u>

- Do something in sports if you have no previous experience

- Go visit anyone who will give you an information interview

- Call before eight and after six

- Research the team from top to bottom – everyone likes their ego stroked

- Make friends with the executive's administrative assistant and receptionist

- Dress as well as you can

- Have a sense of humor
- Ask intelligent and incisive questions if given the chance
- Be prepared to answer the question: what is the most creative project you have ever been involved in?
- Make strong eye contact and have a firm handshake. Lots of jobs are lost in the first 5 seconds.
- Know something about the team owner
- Stop, look, and listen if you get into an office for an interview; see what's on the walls, photos, artwork, etc. It is a great way to bond with the interviewer if you have a common interest
- Take a sales job even if you don't want to sell
- Use every contact you can
- Build a web of contacts
- Bring a resume'
- Be on time!
- Be yourself

No / Don't Do It!

- Spend time talking about your high school sports exploits
- Flap your yap
- Use cynicism or sarcasm in initial meetings
- Hound the interviewer

- Blow your own horn

- Be Late

- Say you hate sales!

- Insert a photo with your resume

- Call their home phone number unsolicited

- Quit

- Fudge your resume

- Check your PDA during the meeting

- Have your phone ring during an interview

- Make excuses

13.) **Chaos and disaster**

Most neophytes in the search process look for the most successful sports teams and leagues they can find and send blind letters to the owner right after they have won a championship. **(Wrong, wrong, wrong.)** You want to reach out to the lepers, disasters, car wrecks, and toxic dumps. Find teams and properties that people are running away from. That's where you want to be.

By pure good luck, my first job in sports was with the Philadelphia 76ers in 1971. For trivia experts they would know that this team had records that stand unbroken to this day. In the '72 – '73 season when I was Administrative Assistant to the GM, we went 9-73. That's right we could not get into double figures in wins. In the same season we had non-contiguous losing streaks of 13, 14, 15, and 20 games.

The longest losing streaks were interrupted by a two point win which, if we had lost, would have given us 33 losses in a row. It was a glorious time in that I was able to take responsibility for areas that I would have had to wait years to experience because the organization was in such disarray. I was learning on the job. Look for chaos, disaster, unrest, change, & opportunity; that is where you are going to learn and move up the fastest.

14.) **If I had only known**

I wish I had known that in most instances there is no major financial equity in the positions that you have in this business. Case in point, Tony Ponturo had been the head of marketing for Anheuser-Busch for many, many years, and one of the more powerful people in sports because of the strength of the A-B brand. As you know, they were taken over by InBev and Tony took a buyout and walked away with many millions of dollars. In pro sports, when a team is sold for "x", the management of that team usually receives a nice gold watch and a pat on the back and is told, "I hope the next owner thinks as highly of you as I did." There is usually no long term equity for employees.

In reality, people always look at the sports side because of the money that the athletes are paid, and if you are at any point of a responsible position in one of those teams, people think that you are in that same salary neighborhood. And again, no complaint, but you are never walking away with a chunk unless ownership has gifted you because of your longevity or brilliance or whatever it might be.

15.) **Enlightening moments**

Hopefully, there have been some or else, wow, have I wasted a lot of time! It was when I was with the Oakland A's in the late 1980s. We were a pretty good baseball team. We were going to the World Series three years in a row. I had been in the business for 14 years and I was having what I guess you would call a crisis of confidence. I was asking what am I doing, why am I in this toy store when there is so much else that could be done in the world, something that would really be giving back to the community, something that was not quite as memorable as working for a pro sports team such as the Oakland A's. I will not say I was ready to go off the proverbial cliff by any stretch, but I was really having doubts about what I had done to that point and what was going to happen next. I had a conversation with my brother - I have two older brothers and my middle brother is a surgeon. I had this heart to heart conversation telling my brother what my questions were and that I didn't think it was very valuable as to what I was doing. He looked at me and he asked me, "How many operations do you think I do in a year?" I said, "I don't know the exact number, but probably several hundred of them are pretty serious." He replied, "Yeah, that's right. And what was your attendance last year?" I said, "2.25 million people."

Then he said, "You don't get it do you?" I answered, "Well, I don't exactly follow what you're trying to get to." He replied, "Most of these people have a good time with their families, with their friends, with their groups. Well, I don't think you should be questioning what you do because you are a part of it. ON the business side and the marketing side, you are providing an opportunity, which is becoming more and more difficult to bring to families, a place where they can come together in a safe and positive environment and enjoy themselves and essentially speak the same language."

For me, that was a moment that has stuck with me to this day. I think it is really important because with the money that is thrown around, the salaries, the-good-the-bad-and-the-ugly of fans, owners, players, front office types, in many instances, your lose that.

Ultimately, no matter what sport you are working in, whether it is pro or college or any other place, what we are doing is bringing

73

the greatest athletes in the world together for fans to celebrate them in what still, in the largest percentage of circumstances, is a positive experience. That conversation enlightened me.

16.) **How I got here**

I would offer some insight based on a recent interview that I was conducting. I asked the candidate, "Tell me about yourself, tell me your story, tell me how you got here." And he said, "By car." Exactly.
MW: Was he serious?

AD: Absolutely serious.

JK: Was he trying to be clever?

AD: Absolutely not. I have a pretty good wise guy meter, but it was one of the best responses that I heard. So I'll say that I got here by car. How did I get here from sitting in Grover Center daydreaming during one of Dr. Owen Wilkinson's classes to watching Mike Schmidt take ground balls at shortstop at that time? I remember saying, "You know, one of these days, he might be a decent minor league player and hopefully some day when I get out of the Sports Administration Program I might actually work for a team and get paid." Little did I know back in the 1970s that Mike Schmidt would turn out to be one of the greatest third basemen in baseball history and, not on any kind of equitable level, that I would end up having a 39-year career in sports, and there we were both in Athens, Ohio, dreaming about the future.

I went from Ohio University to the Philadelphia 76ers to the Maryland Arrows to the Washington Capitals to the Washington Diplomats to the Oakland A's to the Golden State Warriors to my own business consulting group to Tickets.com to the Vancouver / Memphis Grizzlies and today to the San Francisco 49ers. That's kind of a compressed time period of close to four decades, which never ceases to amuse and amaze me, probably more than anybody else. One visual reminder of my whacky ride since 1971 after graduating from Ohio University; I have a plaque on my wall, which has every single one of my business cards along the way. I was the beneficiary of a number of informational interviews way back when as I was going through the internship process at Ohio University and I show that to everybody that comes through here looking for a job in the "high paid, low hour" business of professional sports. I'd say it's not quite as easy as you might think looking at somebody's resume or reading about them or having "Googled" them. Look at this plaque and spend a few moments seeing the different zip codes while I was also trying to raise a family.

MW: Jim or Andy told me you had done that with your business cards and I thought it was great. In order to give readers a clue as to how much they might have to do and where they might have to go, I actually posted that example in part of one of my blog postings.

AD: That is funny. When other people come to the office, everybody looks at it and says, "You know, I need to do one of those." It's not complicated. You don't need a patent to take your business cards and go into "Picture-Frames-R-Us."

JK: Andy has agreed to put that in his will to Ohio University someday unless one of his kids is fighting over it.

AD: Jim, you always bring up these things that I can't quite remember telling you, but whatever you say.

JK: It's my job as the steward of the program.

17.) **Future knowledge**

The ability to multi-task at a level that was not required when we were starting out. At the same time you must have a clear focus that if you get so involved in all your multi-tasking and analyzing all the numbers, you can be pulled further and further away from one of the most important lessons to understand. What is the heart and soul of the organization, the team, the stadium, the college, or whatever it might be? What makes your organization tick?

Every year we are moving at warp speed. The scary part is that even with all of these core competencies, people can do 16 things at once, blindfolded, and upside down. You can lose your way in terms of heart, soul, and head. It is really important to have people understand this in an industry that is maybe becoming more heartless. They have to work harder to understand what is in their own DNA and the DNA of the organization that they are working with, while at the same time working on their Blackberries. I think you better be able to see that evergreen through a snowy forest no matter how many capabilities and abilities, or how much intelligence, or what IQ level you possess.

18.) Jobs, jobs, jobs

This is an overview of the job titles and salary ranges of positions that make up the front offices of most pro sports organizations.

Executive
- Owner
- Chairman
- CEO
- COO – Chief Operating Officer
- President
- Executive Vice President
- Sr. VP Business Operation
- Executive Assistant

- Special Assistant
- Director of Business Development
- Team Legal Counsel
- Receptionist

Team Operations
- President of Team Operations
- General Manager
- Assistant GM
- Director of Player Personnel
- Director of Team Operations
- Director of Scouting
- Scouting Coordinator – College and / or Pro
- Scout
- Head Coach
- Assistant Coach
- Director of Player Development
- Trainer
- Strength and Conditioning Coach
- Assistant Trainer
- Equipment Manager
- Security Director
- Director of Team Travel
- Manager of Team Services
- Director of Team Operations
- Training Facility Manager
- Operations Coordinator
- Team Logistics Manager

Finance

- CFO
- VP Finance
- Controller
- Business Manager
- Accounting Assistant
- Payroll Manager
- Sr. Accountant
- Jr. Accountant
- Finance Director

Community Affairs / Foundations

- Director of Community Affairs
- Director of Community Investment
- Administrative Assistant
- Manager Community Investment
- Community Investment Coordinator
- Coordinator of Youth Development

Marketing Dept.

- CMO - Chief Marketing Officer
- EVP Marketing
- VP Marketing
- Marketing Services Coordinator
- Marketing and Game Operations
- Game Operations Coordinator
- Coordinator of Promotions

- Manager of Event Presentation
- Graphic Designer
- Marketing Coordinator / Sr. Manager of the Internet

Communications and PR

- CCO - Chief Communications Officer
- VP Communications
- Corporate Communications Manager
- Director
- Media Relations Specialist
- Coordinator Publications
- Publications Manager

Arena / Stadium Operation / Facilities

- VP of Operations
- Director of Stadium or Arena Operations
- Ass't. Director of Stadium or Arena Operations
- Project Coordinator
- Facilities Manager
- Coordinator
- Catering Manager
- Merchandising Manager
- Head Groundskeeper
- Parking Manager
- Security Director
- Event Coordinator
- Receptionist

Ticket Sales / Operations and Service

- VP Sales
- VP Service
- Account Executive Sales
- Account Executive Service
- Coordinator Ticket Operations
- Senior Manager Ticket Operations
- Sales Manager
- Service Manager
- Manager Group Sales
- Director Premium Sales
- Box Office Coordinator
- Manager Ticket Services
- Director Guest Services
- Director Ticket Sales Systems

Sponsorship

- VP
- Director of Corporate Sales
- Director of Sponsorship Sales
- Manager of Sponsorship Services
- Manager Business Development
- Client Services Coordinator
- Sponsorship Account Executive
- Administrative Assistant

IT

- Director
- Manager
- Network Coordinator
- Network Engineer

Broadcast Operations

- VP Broadcast
- Video Producer
- Radio Play By Play
- TV Play by Play
- Video Coordinator

Human Resources

- Director
- Coordinator
- Specialist

Miscellaneous

- Mascot
- Preview Center Coordinator
- Website Director
- Dance Team Choreographer
- Warehouse Manager
- Central Services Clerk
- Graphic Design Coordinator
- Team Chaplain
- Alumni Coordinator

Salaries

So now you are lucky enough to snag one of these jobs on an entry level. What can you look forward to? What do people make?
Here is a range of salaries from a typical team sports front office.

$0 – 25,000   17 people
$25,000 – 50,000   59 people
$50,000 – 75,000   26 people
$75,000 – 100,000   11 people
$150,000 – $500,000 7 people
$500,000 and above   4 people

As we like to say in sports, "it beats working for a living."

John Koller - Senior Director, Hardware Marketing at Sony Sony Playstation

Q - What event or series of events were paramount to you breaking into the sports industry?

A- I always heard that you should work where you love, and as a kid, I knew that I loved sports. I would go so far as to audio tape record (in the days when tape recorders were really used) the 49ers' games so that I could listen to the audio from the game again during the week when I got home from school. I simply loved sports, so as a high school kid, I volunteered my time in the Sports Information Department of St Mary's College.

This gave me a wide range of experiences in various sports PR and promotions roles, and really taught me how to write press releases, engage with the media and work with athletes. It was also the impetus to landing a PR internship with the SF 49ers a few years later.

Q- How did you creatively present or package yourself to land the role you are currently in. (interview strategies)

A- My career has really been a series of puzzle pieces that fit, one into the other. My time at St Mary's College in the Sports Information Dept led to a role with the SF 49ers in PR, which led to a role at EA in Marketing, which then led to my current company Sony PlayStation. Ultimately, you need to present yourself well, not only within your resume, but also within interviews. However, I think the most valuable way to market yourself is through others. If you know someone at the company that can speak to the hiring manager in your favor, or can assist via social means such as LinkedIn, this could be as valuable as a successful interview. It's really an important area to consider in today's much more connected, social world.

Q - How would you guide someone in today's market to find the balance of differentiating themselves from other candidates w/out overdoing it?

A - I've always found that the most successful candidates enter the interview with complete research about the company, as well as recommendations for how to solve key issues facing the organization. I had a candidate come to an interview recently with a presentation about themselves without any words – it was all images about what he stood for, why he is the best candidate for the job, and how he would change our organization for the better. Very impressive and much different than the average person who enters our doors looking for a job.

Q - What three or four career search strategies would you advise someone to utilize in today's employment market?

1. Utilize friends and acquaintances for networking. If you receive a positive rep from someone that the hiring manager knows and respects, it goes a very long way.

2. Look for ways to differentiate yourself. Remember that you are a brand. How would you position yourself if given 5 minutes in an elevator with the hiring manager? Everyone comes into a job and says they want it – show the company why you will provide positive ROI from the hire.

3. Search for jobs in industries that you love. Work with people that you love. Don't worry about money as much. Who you work with and what you work on will be much more important in the long run.

Q - Please detail an effective method/technique that someone recently displayed in networking with you.

A- Informational interviews are really smart moves for those who want to find out more about a company or an industry. Find someone that you know and ask for 10-15 minutes. Be prepared to ask questions about the sector – but do not ask for a job during that interview. That's not the time or place. Get the information you're looking for, and follow up after the interview with the fact that you are interested in future opportunities.

Q - Please detail an effective strategy/technique someone utilized on you during an interview process.

A - The presentation noted earlier – was extremely impressive.

Q - What advice or guidance was given to you from a mentor that you would be willing to share?

A - If you ever listen to an athlete after they retire, it's not the game or the money that they miss...it's their teammates and the locker room that they miss. This is similar to all of us non-professional athletes working in the real world. Bottom line – try to work with people you enjoy. It will make all the difference in your career.

Ryan Duey - Director of Marketing & Promotions at University of Michigan

Q - What event or series of events were paramount to you breaking into the sports industry?

A- I volunteered working Full-Time (non-paid) for a few months to show my commitment to the organization.

Q - How did you creatively present or package yourself to land the role you are currently in. (interview strategies)

A- Luck/opportunities always present themselves, but once that opportunity comes about... take the chance, run through it, and never look back.

Q - What three or four career search strategies would you advise someone to utilize in today's employment market?

A- Start networking, and researching some current people in the field and seek advice from them. Show them your interest level in becoming part of their organization, if not the industry as a whole. When opportunities present themselves they will have you in their minds to help you out if you warrant that attention.

Q - Please detail an effective strategy/technique someone utilized on you during an interview process.

A- Interviewed someone a few months back, who had unlimited questions... but what they were asking questions about was upcoming people they were interviewing and the departments they worked in. I completely didn't realize that they were seeking problems and then describing them to that person during the next interview session. They were very tactful with the questions and really impressive throughout the interview process.

Q - What advice or guidance was given to you from a mentor that you would be willing to share?

A -I will only be able to open the door for you... it's up to you to walk through it.

Ryan Leong - Independent Broadcast Professional

Q - What event or series of events were paramount to you breaking into the sports industry?

A- I went to a SF Giants game back in 1991 that was a 'Turn Back the Clock' game. The Giants wore replica 1925 uniforms. It then inspired me to rent the movie 'The Natural' and after watching that film, I became very interested in how the media was portrayed and wanted to be part of that coverage.

Q - How did you creatively present or package yourself to land the role you are currently in.

A- I started as a freelance reporter in late 1998. I picked up various assignments along the way doing updates via the telephone and also interviewing athletes where I would send audio soundbites via telephone and later email to national clients. In 2009, I began working at Metro Networks as a sportscaster and traffic reporter for various Bay Area stations and became more prominent on KCBS serving as a sports and occasional traffic anchor.

Q - How would you guide someone in today's market to find the balance of differentiating himself or herself from other candidate's w/out overdoing it?

A- Everyone has their own style but most important is to find something that makes you, unique. Knowing your subject matter will aid in that differentiation.

Q - What advice or guidance was given to you from a mentor that you would be willing to share?

A- Always be open minded, friendly, and enthusiastic. And strive to continue to learn about your subject matter, whether it's sports, news, or entertainment

Stephanie Gray - Digital Specialist in North America Retail Brand Presentation at Nike.

Q -What event or series of events were paramount to you breaking into the sports industry?

A- I'm a lucky person as I have not only broken through in this industry once but twice. While I strongly believe luck had something to do with it, I also think there is something to be said about persistence, courage and faith.

When I was in college and decided I wanted to be in sports, I was told it would be tough and that I would need a master's degree first. I ignored the person who told me this and went after the job I wanted. I sent out my resume (back when we sent them in the mail instead of online) to as many professional teams I could find contact information for in any town I thought I could live in. Only one person called me out of the 50 to 90 letters I sent out. They told me they didn't have any positions but they had an internship. It was nine months long and in marketing. I really wanted to do PR at the time but I decided it was a foot in the door. So, I moved to a city where I didn't know anyone and took the job. After the internship I got lucky and they had a position open. I applied and was hired on full time. I stayed with that team for eight years. I worked my way up the ladder as far as I could go.

I think this part of my story is important because it isn't just hard to break into the sports industry, but it is hard to move up as well. People stay in their jobs a long time so if you want to grow your career you have to be willing to move sometimes. I did this recently. I left working for a professional team to go work for a large sports company. I sought them out. I went to their website every day looking for positions. I asked my friends and colleagues if they knew anyone at that company. Finally I caught a break when a friend introduced me to his friend who happened to work there. He was nice enough to send out my resume to some colleagues he knew. When they responded to me I drove down to meet them without even knowing if they were hiring. They weren't hiring at the time, but I made an impression so a few months later when my "now boss" posted a job she reached out and asked me to apply. The rest is history.

Jason Jenkins - Director of Media Relations Miami Dolphins

Q - What event or series of events were paramount to you breaking into the sports industry?

A- I was able to break into the sports industry by setting a goal of finding out what a career in sports would entail. I set up informational interviews with people whose career path I wanted to emulate. During college at Texas Tech, I was president of the local chapter of the National Association of Black Journalists. The organization put on a student conference where I booked Dr. Alfonso Scandrett, Jr., who was an Associate Athletics Director to speak at the conference. Dr. Scandrett ultimately became a mentor for me and provided my first opportunity in athletics administration.

Q - How did you creatively present or package yourself to land the role you are currently in.

A- Preparation was the main strategy for my interviews. I didn't want to be generic in terms of how I presented myself. I wanted to find out exactly what the job is for, go through biographies of the people that I am interviewing with and research and understand the organizational philosophy for the organization. You want to build your reputation prior to your visit and use that time to validate the positive impressions that the interviewee has of you before you walk into the door. As I have matured, I have put together detailed portfolio for crisis management, social media and publicity plan documents.

Q - How would you guide someone in today's market to find the balance of differentiating themselves from other candidates w/out overdoing it?

A- Social media and technology have helped potential applications a great deal in the past couple of years. These avenues have allowed potential applications to be able to use ways to connect with potential employers (email, LinkedIn, twitter, etc.) in a way than never before. However, the basic tenets in a job search remain the same. In sports, where the environment is very competitive, it is important to be identify what you want to do early (while you are still in college) and work on getting relevant experience prior to the start of your search.

I also suggest setting up series of informational interviews with people that have careers that you want to emulate. This helps you get your name out in a way to a potential employer in a positive way to build you network. Although a position might not be available during the time you speak with them, they may keep you in mind for a future opportunity at their organization or can you pass your information to their respective contacts.

89

Q - What three or four career search strategies would you advise someone to utilize in today's employment market?

A- Look at yourself as a brand. How you present yourself is paramount to how you are perceived online and in person. After receiving a resume for a potential applicant, the first thing I do is a Google search and see how they present themselves on their Facebook and Twitter pages. This is important to me in public relations because the person that we hire will be come across sensitive information in this job and we want to make sure that person is mature enough to handle this information. How they present themselves digitally is important in determining this.

Jennifer Cingari - Publicist, ESPN

When you walk into a job interview, your goal is to stand out among the other candidates. Most people do this by talking; explaining their experience and speaking about their strengths. But it's even more important to show you're the best candidate.

One way to creatively present yourself is to build a portfolio of your work. Spend time choosing writing samples or items that show your experience as it relates to the job you're applying for. By providing examples of press releases I wrote, along with the newspaper articles that came from that work, I could back up what I was saying with actual documents. Plus, they were able to see my writing style and the effectiveness of my work all put together in a neat leather binder (don't forget the sheet protectors!)

To go a step further, build off of your portfolio by picking your 3-5 best pieces and make a small packet to leave with your interviewer. It will give them something to read and hang on to after the interview is completed—leaving you at the front of their mind!

Pat Gallagher - Sports Marketing Pioneer

Q- What event or series of events were paramount to you breaking into the sports industry?

A- In 1976 I was named the San Francisco Giants first Director of Marketing. At the time, I was one of only a few in MLB with that title. A few enlightened team owners realized that aside from just providing information, access and perks (food/booze/ travel) to sportswriters and simple promotions like "Ladies Day", Businessman's Special" and "Little League Day", it made sense to find new ways to reach out to fans, sponsors and the community in a creative and pro-active fashion.

My background was not in sports, but in various management roles in the theme park business with Sea World and Marine World/Africa USA, which began as an hourly seasonal employee when I was in high school. Theme parks like Sea World and Disneyland were seen as leaders in creative family entertainment, aggressive promotion and customer service, all things professional sports was seeking. New Giants owner Bob Lurie who stepped in at the 11th hour to save the Giants from moving to Toronto made me one of his first new hires in the front office.

Q - How did you creatively present or package yourself to land the role you are currently in?

A- I was part of a small group of executives recruited from Disney and Sea World to help turn around a regional attraction, Marine World/Africa USA on the San Francisco peninsula. I received some credit for my work there and was asked to interview for the newly created position with the Giants. After interviewing with Mr. Lurie, he offered me the job.

Q - How would you guide someone in today's market to find the balance of differentiating himself or herself from other candidate's w/out overdoing it?

A - Be yourself. People don't hire slick resumes, they hire people who have left a positive impression. Find succinct ways to answer these questions: "What have I done that qualifies me for this opportunity?" and "Why should you hire me for this job?" Be prepared to demonstrate how you helped solved a few business problems in the past. Don't brag, but be confident and open. Listen to the interviewers questions before answering.

Be conservative in your dress and appearance, be on time, and be earnest and positive. Remember that not only are they interviewing you; you are interviewing them. Ask good questions. Follow up with a note or email to let them know of your interest.

Q - What three or four career search strategies would you advise someone to utilize in today's employment market.

A- Manage your personal contact network effectively. Use each interview as not only a way to sharpen your interviewing skills, but as valuable contacts for future opportunities. I've referred many times more people than I have ever hired. I think it is good business to help those who have impressed even in informational interviews. It helps reinforce my network with people I trust. Nobody but you will convince them to hire you, but sometimes your network can be valuable to help get you in the door or say a few words about you.

Do your homework. Become informed about your target company, the key personnel, recent news, history and competition. It shows respect and initiative.

Don't make the mistake of overkill with people calling on your behalf particularly before you have been asked for references. It reeks of desperation and can backfire.

Q - Please detail an effective method/technique that someone recently displayed in networking with you.

A- A job seeker who I didn't hire, but was impressed with, asked if they could stay in touch with me and specifically asked what would be the most convenient way for me to have them do so.

Q - Please detail an effective strategy/technique someone utilized on you during an interview process.

A- A candidate did enough homework to understand what challenges we were facing. Without assuming they had the right answers, they offered a few suggested approaches and admitted that although their ideas might be off the mark, they wanted to demonstrate how they think and what their approach might be. Gave me a snapshot of the candidate's ability and personality.

Q - What advice or guidance was given to you from a mentor that you would be willing to share?

A- A couple of words of wisdom from several wise people: "You learn way more about people with how they behave during the bad times than you do with how they behave during the good times." "There are only two kinds of people: problem solvers and problem creators. Be regarded as a problem solver."

One of the best quotes from Mark Twain: "If you tell the truth, you don't need to remember anything."

Pat Gallagher, one of the longest serving executives in San Francisco Giants history is credited with being among the most creative marketing and business minds in professional sports, entertainment and the visitor industry during his 40-year career.

After leaving the Giants, in 2010 he formed Gallagher & Associates to focus on management consulting and concept development in professional sports, technology, entertainment and the visitor/hospitality industries. Pat currently serves on the San Francisco America's Cup Organizing Committee, is co-founder and vice chairman of San Francisco's annual Kraft "Fight Hunger" Bowl (formerly the Emerald Bowl), board member of Martin Resorts, and the Bay Area Sports Hall of Fame.

Gallagher capped off his 33 year stint as the top marketing/business and "idea guy" for the Giants as president of Giants Enterprises LLC, a subsidiary of the Giants coinciding with the opening of Pacific Bell Park (now AT&T Park) to develop profitable non-baseball ventures and business opportunities for the organization.

He was a major contributor to the design and development of the Giants acclaimed waterfront ballpark, creating the park's original marketing plan, securing the naming rights, key corporate partnerships and establishment of the Charter Seat License concept which were foundational elements required to make the first privately financed major league ballpark in over 30 years a reality.

As the Giants senior vice president/business operations during 23 of the "Candlestick Park years," Gallagher gained national recognition for promotional flair with legendary thematic marketing campaigns aimed at selling tickets and generating a personality for the notoriously cold and windy ballpark. The "Croix de Candlestick" decoration for fans braving the elements, "Crazy Crab" the anti-mascot, Circus Wallenda high-wire sky walk, "Ball Dudes," Fog Horn and baseball's first full-time female PA announcer, classic uniform and brand elements were among the most notable of Gallagher's contributions.

Overtime
The 4 C Rule of Communications:

Be Clear

Be Concise

Be Confident

Have a call to action

Here is another set of four basic rules to keep in mind when as you navigate your career search strategy.

Be Clear:

It is crucial to be clear with your words both in writing and verbally when you are communicating with someone. Sounds pretty basic right? You would be surprised how many sports industry hopefuls do not craft together a clear message when they are networking, in an informational interview and most scary, while in a live interview. Being clear is different than being scripted or too rehearsed in your words. What is important is that you are able make a point in a decisive manner.

The toughest class I took in college was a public speaking class. We were asked to not only deliver numerous speeches to our classmates but they were recorded on video as well. We then had to endure the discomfort of watching it and seeing for ourselves how awkward our body language was, how often we used filler words like, um, ah, like, etc.

Practice, it will seem odd at first but practice your positioning statement while you are driving the car, while you are exercising, in the shower, wherever and whenever you have a few minutes of quiet time. Remember, do not rehearse it so that it sounds robotic, just practice it until it rolls off your tongue naturally and in a conversational manner.

Be Concise:

Far too often I am on phone calls or in F2F (face-to-face) meetings where it seemingly takes forever for someone to get to their key points and make their points stand out. With today's average attention span being as short as it is, it is important to make every effort to be concise with our message. Depending on the scenario, keeping your messaging concise will almost always benefit you. Once you have a meeting, an informational interview or phone call already set, when the meeting gets going, this is the time to be concise.

Be Confident:

Finding the right balance of being humble and being down right arrogant can be a challenge. There is nothing wrong with being confident when you are talking about yourself, your background and your positioning statement. Just be mindful that a little confidence can go a long way to helping you. Too much confidence will more than likely be perceived as arrogance and that is tough to overcome. Accenting your key points with how you like to learn will show two elements. That you are a confident person (good) as well as someone who likes to enhance their skill set (even better).

Call to Action:

During the initial phase of networking or going out on informational meetings, it is very important to always end the conversation with a call to action. What is a call to action?

Simply put, what do you want to ask the person you are meeting with, or on the phone with? Do you want to meet them in person, do you want to set a time to ask them a few very specific questions? Would you like them to refer you to one of their contacts?

Whatever it is you want out of the meeting or call, make it known by asking. There are a lot of nice ways to ask a question, such as; I see that you are connected with Steve Smith, would you be open to making a brief introduction on my behalf?

About the Author

With more than 19 years in the sports industry and in corporate America, Matt Crevin combines his practical, real world experiences...with his insider sports knowledge and industry connections directly to you, an industry hopeful.

His career kicked off in 1991 as a "rookie" public relations intern for the San Francisco 49ers. He played an important role with the football team by:

Setting up post game player interviews with the national media Working directly with the players on their community events, providing inside information from the press box, on game day, to some of the biggest names in NFL broadcasting.

Over the next decade, his skills and experience with the national media grew and his role with the 49ers evolved into a highly specialized sports position, which included:

Radio and television coverage of home 49er games from the booth, sidelines and locker room

Spotting for select West Coast NFL games as a member of the Westwood One/CBS radio team, working side-by-side with sports broadcast greats, such as Al Michaels, John Madden, the late Harry Kalas, Dick Enberg, and Marv Albert – to name just a few.

Today, Matt continues his business and personal relationship with the 49ers as the press box public address announcer. He has lived through the ups and downs, highs and lows and all the behind-the-scenes action of an NFL dynasty, as only an insider can see.

Equipped with business background and sports insider's knowledge, Matt shares his passion and knowledge with his clients. He delivers to his individual clients a unique process and format, which gives sports industry hopefuls a unique look into the numerous career opportunities available in the sports industry and most important, how to create a career search strategy. His experience and perspective are not found or learned in college, it only comes through years of experience and networking, all geared to bring you results.

What Others Are Saying

"When I first met Matt I was a college student looking to get into the sports industry. He was instrumental in helping me understand the value of networking, and helped me build a network of my own with other sports professionals. Now that I have work in the sports industry full-time, I can fully appreciate the lessons he shared and realize the positive impact he had on my career. *-Michael I. NBA Ticket Sales Representative*

"Matt did a great job of connecting with the students at Iowa State University. To be able to hear from someone with more than 18 years of experience in the sports industry and corporate world was an excellent opportunity for the students."
Tammy Stegman
Career Coordinator for Marketing and Management
Business Career Services | Iowa State

"Matt has written a book that should be a valuable resource for those looking to breaking into the field of sports & media. His background in business and NFL media relations gives him a unique perspective to share with readers. There are more jobs in sports then you can imagine, and Matt's experiences should serve you well as you try to open your own doors."
Damon Bruce, KNBR Radio San Francisco

"I sat in on a presentation delivered by Matt Crevin of Voice of the Box and by far, it was one of the best career decisions I have made. His presentation to Sam Houston State University was a great success and I quickly reached out to retain Matt as my career coach. His career coaching was value packed, right to the point and provided me the guidance and tools I have implemented to land my first job in the baseball industry. I would not be in the position I am in today without Matt's top-level coaching services. I encourage anyone, who is looking to break into the sports industry to connect with Matt, you will not be disappointed!" *-Roy Johnson*

"I knew I wanted to work in the sports industry, but was uncertain in which direction to go to get that opportunity. After going through Matt's 4 step coaching process and him introducing me to many techniques used in the sports industry, I knew I was headed in the right direction and was anxious to get out and connect with people within the industry."

"No matter if it was an intern or the general manager of a sports franchise, when seeking advice Matt gave me the confidence to reach out and network with anyone in the sports industry."

"I credit Matt and his coaching services for helping me establish and keep a lot of the connections within the sports industry I have today."

"Through out the coaching process Matt was always willing to make time for me even with his busy schedule, no matter if it was early in the morning or late in the evening. Even though our coaching sessions are done now Matt still reaches out to me to check on things, and its something I always appreciate."
-C. Hayes

18693514R00061

Made in the USA
Lexington, KY
19 November 2012